School RULES!

projects

planning and polishing pointers
to make you a project pro

by Emma MacLaren Henke
illustrated by Nikki Upsher

WILD ANIMAL
HAB

Published by American Girl Publishing

No part of this book may be used or reproduced in any manner whatsoever without written permission except in the case of brief quotations embodied in critical articles and reviews.

17 18 19 20 21 22 23 24 LEO 10 9 8 7 6 5 4 3 2 1

Editorial Development: Darcie Johnston
Art Direction & Design: Sarah Jane Boecher
Production: Jeannette Bailey, Caryl Boyer, Cynthia Stiles, Kristi Tabrizi
Illustrations: Nikki Upsher
Special thanks to Tanya Zempel, elementary education consultant

Library of Congress Cataloging-in-Publication Data
Names: Henke, Emma MacLaren, author. | Upsher, Nikki, illustrator.
Title: School rules! Projects : planning and polishing pointers to make you a project pro /
by Emma MacLaren Henke ; illustrated by Nikki Upsher.
Description: Middleton, WI : American Girl Publishing, 2017. | Series: School rules!
Identifiers: LCCN 2016025587 (print) | LCCN 2016044404 (ebook) |
ISBN 9781683370017 (pbk.) | ISBN 9781683370048 (ebook) | ISBN 9781683370048 (epub)
Subjects: LCSH: Report writing—Juvenile literature. | Research—Juvenile literature. |
Girls—Life skills guides—Juvenile literature.
Classification: LCC LB1047.3 .H46 2017 (print) | LCC LB1047.3 (ebook) | DDC 808.02—dc23
LC record available at https://lccn.loc.gov/2016025587

 americangirl.com/service

Dear Reader,

School projects can feel like a very big deal. When you're faced with a research report to write, a model to make, or a presentation to prepare, it's hard to know where to start.

Whatever kind of project you're working on, the secret to success (and to keeping your cool) is making a plan. This book will guide you step-by-step, whether you're reporting on wild animal habitats, dressing like an ancient Egyptian, or staging a super science experiment. You'll discover the best ways to keep track of your ideas, your materials, and your time. You'll learn how to brainstorm and choose topics. You'll find tips for doing research and advice for getting the right kind of help.

Projects let your creative side shine. They let you learn by doing and by exploring your own interests. Best of all, you can have fun along the way! We'll show you how.

Your Friends at American Girl

contents

· PAGE 66 ·
INFORMATION, PLEASE!

Find and manage the facts you need
for a top-notch project.

· PAGE 80 ·
THE FINISH LINE

Polish your project, work with a team,
and solve project problems.

THE PROJECT PROCESS

Follow these steps to make a plan for any project assignment.

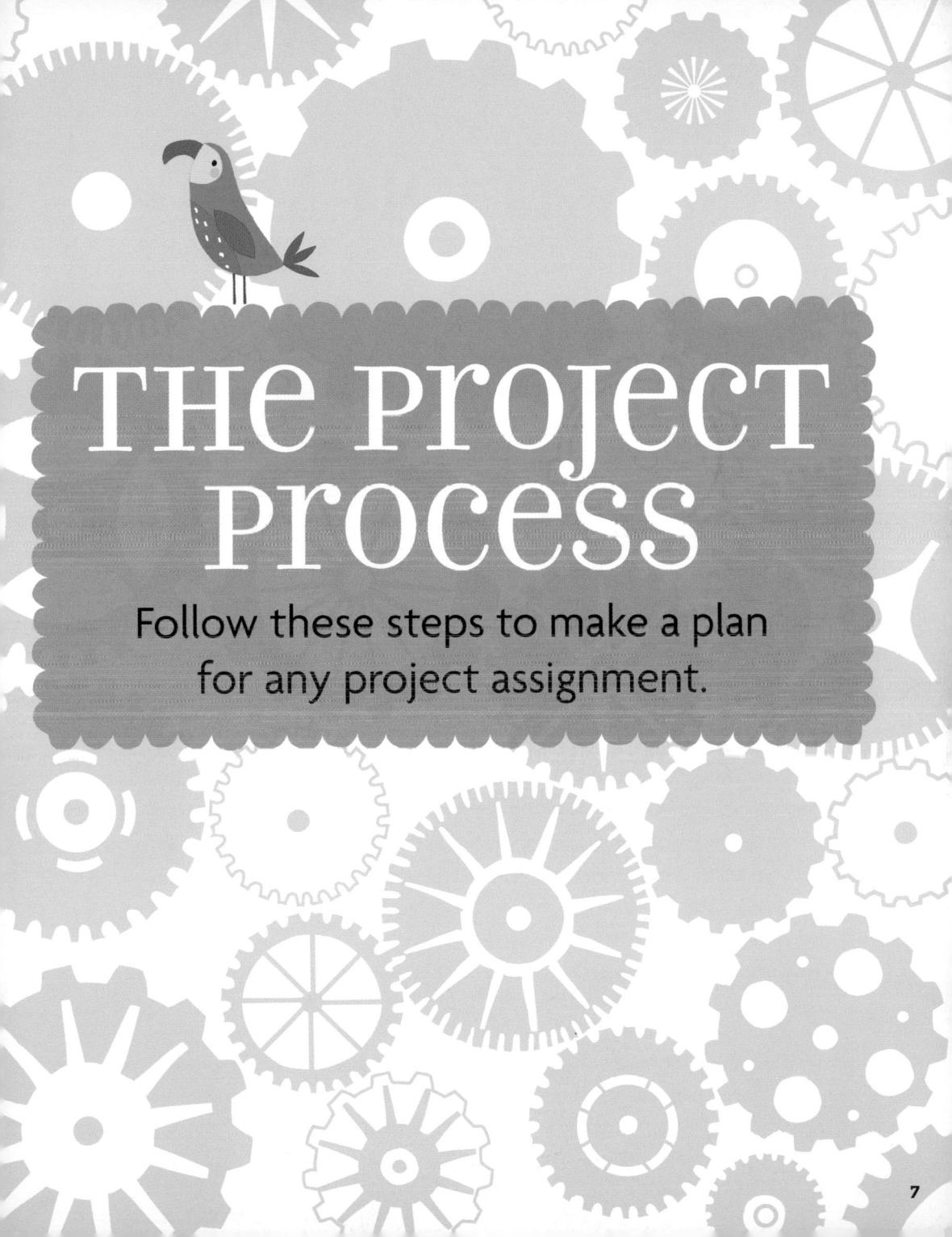

MOTIVATION METER

What's your attitude toward tackling tough projects?

1. This morning, your teacher handed out the assignment sheet for a five-page report due in three weeks. By lunchtime you've . . .
   a. made a list of possible topics and a daily plan for completing the report on time.
   b. started to think about a topic.
   c. stuffed the assignment sheet in your locker. You don't need it yet—three weeks is far away!

2. Thinking about the six book reports due by Thanksgiving makes you feel . . .
   a. excited! You've read some great books, and you've already got four done.
   b. a little nervous. You've read some great books, but you've got to figure out what to write.
   c. completely overwhelmed. You haven't even visited the library, and the due date is less than a month away.

3. Your teacher asks for your help planning a class celebration. You begin by . . .
   a. brainstorming themes and recruiting friends to make snacks.
   b. asking your friends what they think the party should be like.
   c. dreaming about the delicious party food. Mmm . . . pizza!

4. You're working on a group project for history class: a skit about the American Revolution. When it's one week till showtime, you've made sure your group has . . .
   a. written the skit, made the costumes, and memorized lines.
   b. come up with a clever skit. Now you need to assign the parts and learn the lines.
   c. had fun working on the project. You haven't gotten much done on the skit, but you and your pals are now champs at your dad's vintage pinball machine.

5. You decided to dress up as Marie Curie for the science fair, but your outfit's not turning out as you planned. You decide to . . .

a. ask your parents and school librarian for help. If the librarian steers you in the right direction, your mom can help you sew a cool costume.

b. borrow a lab coat from your neighbor who's a pharmacist and ask your mom to help you find pictures of Marie Curie.

c. throw on one of your dad's white shirts, pretend it's a lab coat, and call it a day.

Answers

Give yourself 3 points for each **a** answer you chose, 2 points for each **b**, and 1 point for every **c**, and add up your score.

12–15
A+ PROJECT PREPPER

8–11
MAKING PROJECT PROGRESS

5–7
PROJECT PROCRASTINATOR

However you score, if you plan your time and break your project down into small tasks, you can complete any assignment with success. Tend to dawdle or delay when you're faced with a challenging project? You're not alone! Try these tactics to get up to speed and keep at it till you reach the finish line.

Use a calendar to organize your tasks, and check off the days as they pass.

Ask a family member or friend to keep you on track.

Break your project down into small steps. Reward yourself—call a friend, pet your cat, have a treat—after each step you complete.

Use to-do lists. Check off each item after you do it—and enjoy the sense of satisfaction!

Set aside a specific time each day to work and review your progress.

KNOW BEFORE YOU GO

The best way to begin? Read the directions, highlighting the four kinds of info you need to know.

Social Studies
Unit 3
Ms. Cronos

Greek God or Goddess Research Project

To conclude our study of Greek mythology, your assignment is to research a Greek god or goddess who interests you and create a report that includes a class presentation.

You'll write a 300- to 500-word report about your god or goddess, accompanied by a visual presentation of your research, such as a poster, slide show, model, or costume.

Be ready to present your project in class on Monday, February 23. You'll summarize your report in a one-minute speech and share your visual presentation.

Big Picture

This is what you're supposed to do and what you'll turn in when you're done.

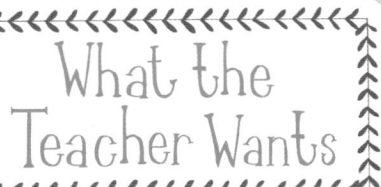
What the Teacher Wants

Look for the specific details about different parts of the assignment.

- How long should your report be?
- What items do you need to include?
- What should your project look like?

Examples

You can use your teacher's suggestions, but don't be afraid to be creative. Check with your teacher if you have questions about your idea.

Due Date

Write your project due date in your planner as soon as you get the assignment. Sometimes teachers set separate due dates for different parts of the project. Be sure to mark each one.

As you work on your project, check the assignment details every few days—not just at the beginning and the end. That way you can be sure you're doing all the right things and keeping up the pace. If there's a detail you're not sure about, ask your teacher instead of guessing. Teachers want you to succeed!

LIGHTNING STRIKES!

Spark ideas for your project with brainstorming.

When you **brainstorm,** you write down whatever ideas come to mind during a short period of time—just 5 or 10 minutes. Don't judge! Simply write every thought down. When you're done, pick out the ideas you like best.

Here are three different ways to brainstorm. Use them all to choose your general topic, and then pinpoint a specific idea for your project.

LIST IT

To choose a topic, just write all your ideas in a list. If you like, add a few words about why each idea interests you. Then look at your list and decide which idea appeals to you the most.

Zeus
he's in charge

Athena
wisdom—that's cool
helped heroes
city of Athens

Aphrodite
goddess of love

~~Janus two faces~~
~~Do I have to write~~
~~two reports?~~
oops!
NOT GREEK
can't do anyway

Artemis
goddess of hunt
bow & arrow?
animals—
I love animals!

Map It

After you've chosen a topic, use it to make a mind map. Start by writing your topic in the middle of a blank sheet of paper and circling it. Then write thoughts *about* the topic around it. Use lines to connect any thoughts that are related to each other. Include ideas, facts, and even questions in your mind map—they will help guide your research later on.

Why is olive tree so important for Athens?

owl

could make a good drawing

olive tree

symbol

goddess of wisdom

Parthenon

reason and justice

Athena

Athens

goddess of warfare

favorite daughter of Zeus

sprang from his head?!

goddess of weaving, pottery, crafts

She helped Greek heroes. Why?

QUESTION IT

Now brainstorm a list of questions that you'd like to answer about your topic, starting with the basics:

WHO?
Greek goddess or god—Athena. Also, who were her friends and enemies among the other gods?

WHAT?
Goddess of wisdom, war. What else did she represent?

WHERE?
Ancient Greece. Was she worshipped anyplace else?

WHEN?
A long time ago!!! (In what years did ancient Greeks worship her most?)

HOW?
How did she get her powers? How did she help heroes?

WHY?
Why was she so popular and adored?

Jot down answers if you know them, and use unanswered questions as a starting point for your research.

Here's another important question: WHAT DO I WANT TO KNOW MORE ABOUT?

If you're interested in your topic, you'll have fun working on your project. And if you care about your topic, your teacher and classmates will probably care, too.

When you're sure of your topic, come up with a final question that helps you pinpoint the main idea of your project. Here are some examples . . .

Why was Athena so important to the people of Athens?

How did Athena become associated with olives, owls, and her other symbols?

How did the other gods see Athena? How did she fit in among them?

THE RIGHT IDEA

Answer these questions to make sure your topic is *juuust* right.

~~Greek goddesses~~

300–500 words? I could only say a little bit about a few goddesses.

Is it too broad? Is there too much info to fit in my project?

~~Athena's owl~~

How much can I really find out about this bird?

Athena's Owl

Is it too narrow? Will I run out of things to say?

~~Athena is the goddess of wisdom.~~

um, nothing new here.

Is it too simple? Will I just be saying what people already know?

Why was Athena so important to Athens?

Wisdom Courage strength

THIS IS IT!

Will it let me ask questions and discover new things, or just list facts?

Why is this such a good topic? Because it allows you to give general information about Athena but also find out something more: the reasons why the goddess was so important to the people of ancient Athens. It also lets you form ideas and opinions, and it gives readers a chance to form them, too.

DIVIDE AND CONQUER

Break down your project into steps,
and then set a schedule for completing each one.

As soon as you receive the assignment, read through it carefully and find out exactly what you need to do. Make a list of the parts.

Next, make a list of supplies you'll need. Gather what you have, and ask your parents or teacher for help getting the rest.

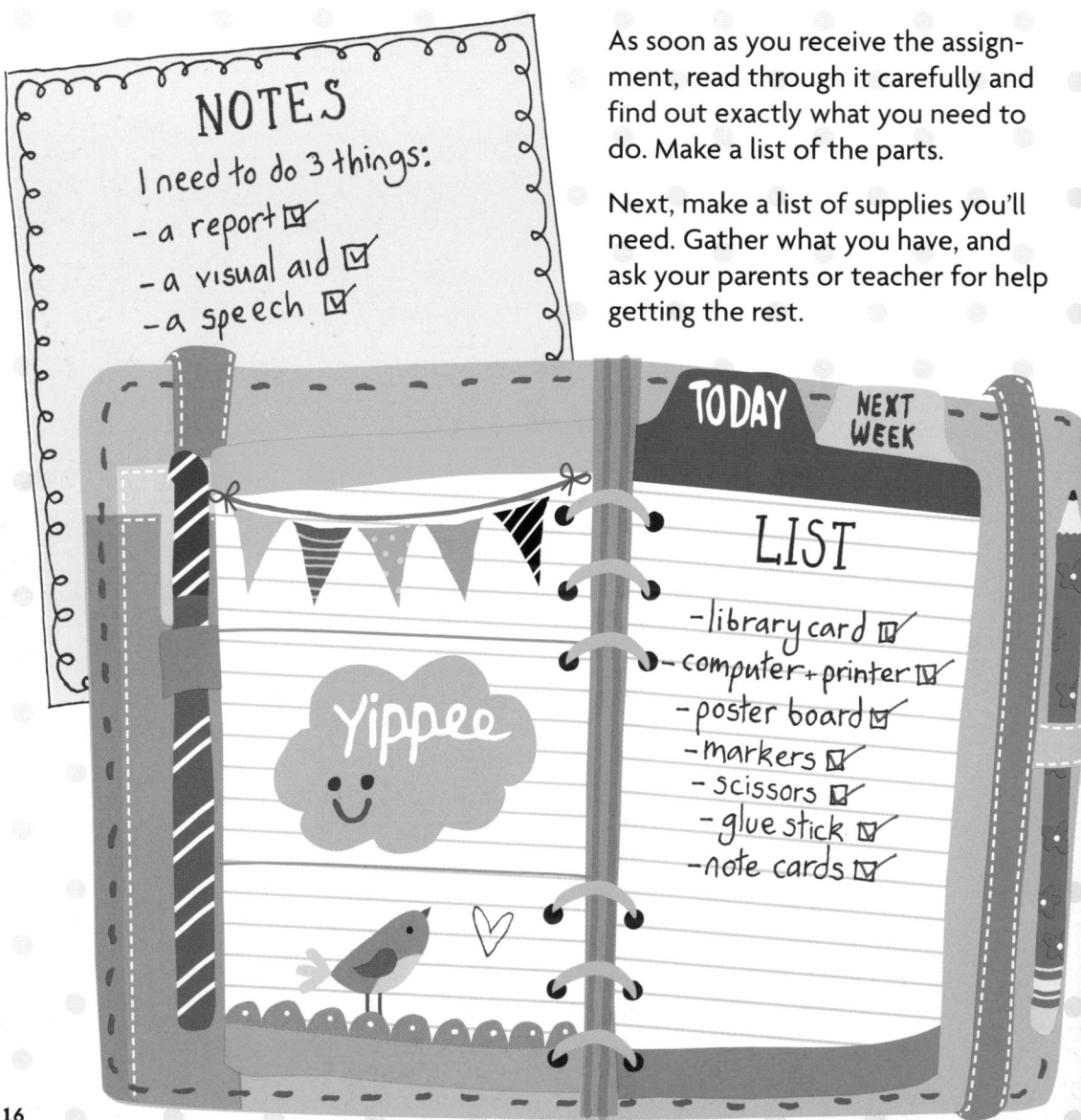

Mark the due date on your calendar or planner. Then, working backward from that date, schedule the smaller steps you'll take to complete your project.

BRAINSTORM: Generate and refine your ideas. Come up with questions that you'll research.

RESEARCH: Read books, online articles, and other sources. Take notes and organize them. Try to find answers to your research questions. Figure out how the information you find fits into your project.

CREATE: Draft your report, lay out your poster, write your speech, build your model.

REVIEW, EDIT & PRACTICE:

Give yourself time to review your work. Edit and proofread your writing, practice your performance, and put finishing touches on posters and models.

S	M	T	W	T	F	S
1	2 brainstorm ideas and questions	3 decide project topic	4	5 visit library, find resources	6 search for online resources	7
8 review research and take notes	9 review research and take notes	10	11 outline report	12 write report draft	13 write report draft	14
15 find images and lay out poster	16 edit report draft	17 Dad help proofread report?	18 make speech note cards	19 practice speech	20 practice speech	21
22 practice speech and poster presentation	23 Goddess Project Due!	24	25	26	27	28

FEBRUARY

WHAT'S YOUR PROJECT POWER?

Report? Speech? Model? Poster? Sometimes your teacher lets you choose! Which project style suits you best?

1. At school, one subject where you're a star student is . . .
   a. public speaking. Your speech style sets a high bar.
   b. art. Your paintings and sculptures earn great grades.
   c. English. You love writing essays, stories, and book reports.

2. Your mom needs your help getting ready for your family reunion. You'd volunteer to . . .
   a. write a letter urging far-flung relatives to make the trip.
   b. create a scrapbook that highlights all the branches of your brood.
   c. plan a skit about your family's talents, hobbies, and quirks.

3. The after-school activity that calls your name is . . .
   a. improv comedy club.
   b. writer's workshop.
   c. pottery studio.

4. You'd enjoy earning a scout badge called . . .
   a. Creative Crafter: you could sew, make jewelry, and model with clay.
   b. Drama Dreamer: you could perform a soliloquy, dress in costume, and write a skit.
   c. Story Scout: you could write a short story and start a troop book group.

5. You want to create a special surprise for your best friend's birthday. You'd decide to . . .
   a. knit a scarf in her favorite color.
   b. write her a personalized poem.
   c. prep all your pals to perform a singing telegram birthday wish.

answers

Did you choose mostly **blue?** Your project power is writing. That's a superpower, because most projects require you to research and write at least a little.

BRANCH OUT!

Tired of reports and posters? Try these creative ways to show what you know!

★ Build a board game.

★ Write and perform a skit.

★ Produce your own digital video.

★ Showcase photos you take yourself in a collage or slide show.

★ Create a crossword or word search.

★ Construct a diorama.

Did you go with mostly **green?** Your project power is creating. You'd choose hands-on projects that let you make models, costumes, dioramas, posters, and more. Try planning your steps to "build" reports and speeches the same way you plan the projects you craft or create.

Did you pick **purple** the most? Your project power is performing. When you can, you like to present projects as a speech, skit, or show. You can use your performer's polish to perk up reports, posters, and models, too.

Many school projects call on all three powers. Make the most of your top strength, but don't be afraid to try something new. School projects teach you as much about planning and working on your own as they do about the subject you study.

STOCK UP!

Keep these supplies on hand for a head start on any project.

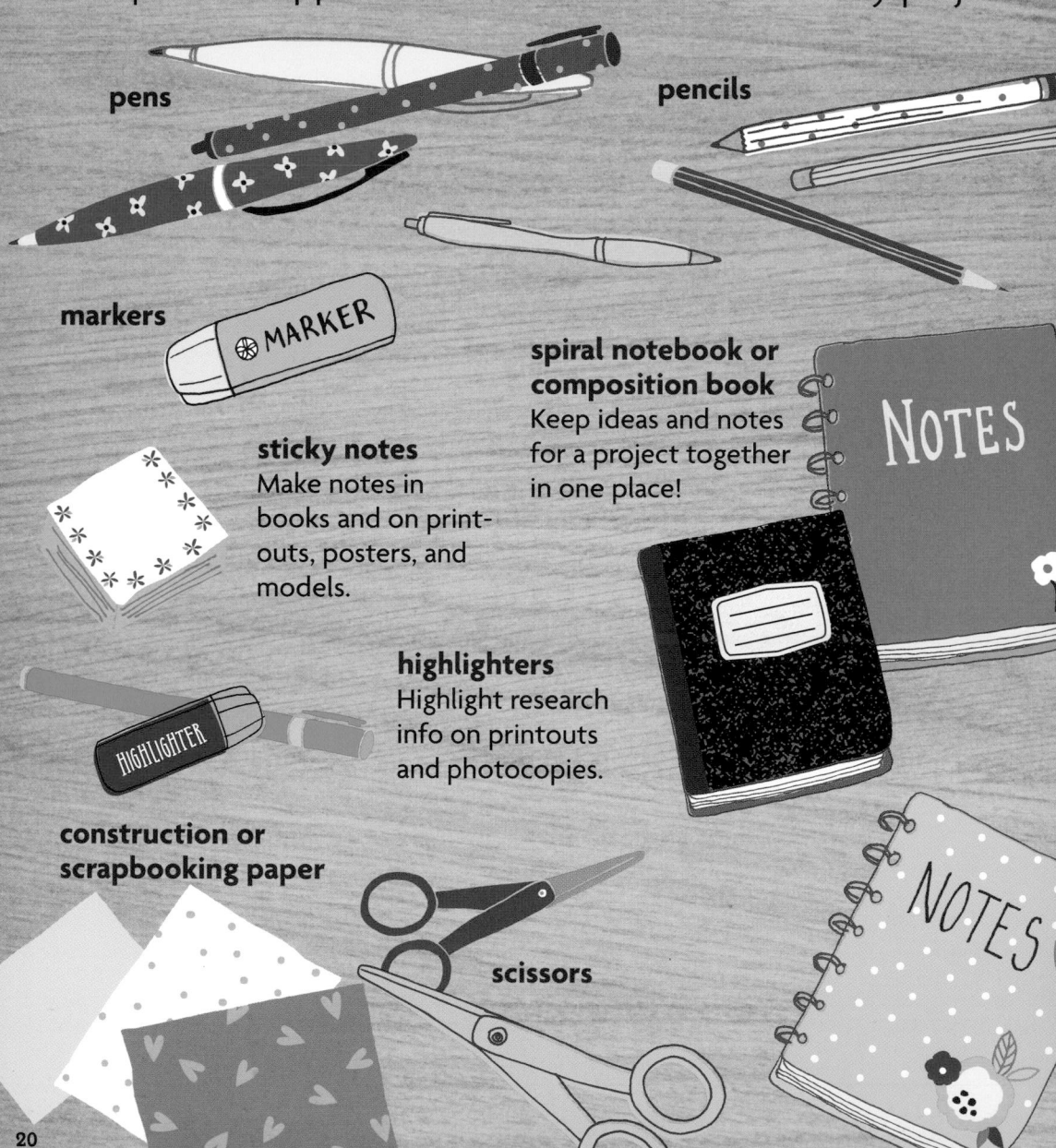

pens

pencils

markers

MARKER

sticky notes
Make notes in books and on print-outs, posters, and models.

spiral notebook or composition book
Keep ideas and notes for a project together in one place!

NOTES

highlighters
Highlight research info on printouts and photocopies.

HIGHLIGHTER

construction or scrapbooking paper

scissors

NOTES

ruler
Cut along a straight edge. Measure perfect placement for poster images.

tape

note cards
Use them for taking notes and giving presentations.

paper

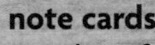

computer and printer
If you don't have them at home, use them at your school or library.

library card
Your most important project tool!

glue sticks

GLUE STICK

GLUE STICK

LIBRARY CARD

1 2 4 7 8 1 2

poster board

REALITY CHECK

Can you tell if your big idea is *too* big?
Ask yourself these **questions** to find out.

What do I already know, and what will I be able to learn?

Your project is a presentation on American Sign Language. But you don't know any sign language yourself. You'd plan to . . .

a. teach your classmates how to tell a joke in sign language.

b. show your class how to spell your name and say please and thank you in sign language.

How much time do I have?

You're writing fiction for English, and you have a great story idea. Your next writing project is due in three weeks. You'd decide to . . .

a. expand your idea into a multi-chapter novel.

b. use your idea to write and polish a 1,000-word short story.

What supplies do I need, and how much will they cost?

You need to build a model of an Egyptian pyramid for your world history class. You'd decide to . . .

a. ask your mom to take you to the toy store to buy that detailed gold-block pyramid building set you saw on TV. It costs $199.99, but wow! It will be so beautiful when it's done.

b. figure out what you can do with heavy-duty cardboard from the recycling bin and gold paint from the garage.

> **Who else do I need to involve, and how will I organize their help?**

Your teacher wants you to "perform" a book report. You'd choose to . . .

a. stage a scene from your book that takes place at a crowded party. You'll recruit all your classmates to act as extras!

b. memorize a monologue from the main character of your book and recite it in class.

> **Where will I get help if I need it?**

Time for the science fair. You'd plan to research . . .

a. brain chemistry. You live in a university town, and you know there's a brain science lab on campus. They'll let you in and help with your project, right?

b. which materials are the best conductors of electricity. Your mom is an electrical engineer, so she should be able to help.

Answers

Did you choose any **a's?** If so, you might need a reality check! Before you invest your time or money in a project, review the **questions** to make sure your idea is one you can handle. Don't get in over your head!

REDUCE, REUSE, RECYCLE

Keep project costs down by searching for supplies around the house. Check out . . .

closets and costume bins. Dressing up as Bessie Coleman? See if you can borrow your dad's leather bomber jacket and your brother's swim goggles. Clara Barton? Maybe you could wear the lab coat from your mad scientist Halloween costume.

the family craft bin. Jazz up your poster or model with glitter glue, felt cutouts, and even feathers!

the recycling bin. Heavy cardboard boxes make sturdy backing material for posters. Cut, glue, and paint cardboard shapes to make architectural models.

the toy box. Use interlocking blocks to create custom models. Use toy animals, action figures, or doll furniture in dioramas.

gift wrap. Use wrapping paper as a poster background. Tissue paper, ribbons, and bows can enhance costumes, too.

PROJECTS THAT SHINE

Get tips to ace any kind of project, from reports and posters to models and speeches.

Reasoned Research Reports

Support your ideas with evidence to tell a convincing story.

Writing a research report is a lot like telling a story. You need a beginning, a middle, and an end. And you need to make sure readers can follow your thoughts at each point along the way.

MIDDLE

BEGINNING

END

Start with an **introduction** that tells your readers the main idea of your report and why that idea is interesting or important. In other words, tell them what you're going to tell them! To grab their attention from the first sentence, try beginning with a quote, question, or interesting fact.

opening question

main idea

Athena and Athens

Did you know that the Parthenon, the most famous monument of ancient Greece, is a temple to the goddess Athena? The ancient Athenians worshipped and admired Athena for many reasons. As the goddess of wisdom, she stood for something that Athenians were proud of. As the goddess of war, she fought for justice, which the Athenians believed in. And according to Greek mythology, Athena gave the olive tree to the city of Athens so that she could become the city's goddess.

Athena competed with Poseidon, the Greek god of the seas, to become the god who represented Athens. Both gods gave the city a gift. Poseidon created a fountain of salt water. It was

Fill the middle—or **body**—of your report with **evidence** that supports your main idea. Your assignment may tell you how many examples, reasons, or facts to provide. If your teacher doesn't give you specific guidelines, though, try to include at least three pieces of evidence.

evidence (reasons, examples, or facts)

Athena competed with Poseidon, the Greek god of the seas, to become the god who represented Athens. Both gods gave the city a gift. Poseidon created a fountain of salt water. It was pretty, but the people could not drink from it or use the water to grow plants. Athena gave the city the olive tree. Her gift provided food, wood, oil, and other things.

Athens was the center of learning for ancient Greece. It makes sense that people of the city would admire the goddess of wisdom. Mythology says that Athena used her wisdom to create or inspire some of the most useful skills and tools in ancient Greece, such as weaving and pottery. Athenians relied on Athena's gifts every day.

As the goddess of war, Athena inspired the Athenians to use their minds to win battles and other contests. Athena stood for fighting wars for just reasons, not for the sake of battle. Athenians believed in fighting wars for justice.

At the end—or **conclusion**—of your report, restate your main idea. Then review or summarize the evidence and answer any remaining questions. For an ending that is interesting and strong, make a final point or remind your readers of the beginning of the report.

restatement of main idea

Athena was loved by the people of Athens for many reasons. She gave the city the olive tree, an important resource. She was wise, and ancient Athenians valued wisdom. She fought for justice and with reason, as the people of Athens hoped to do. The Athenians admired their city's goddess so much that they built a huge temple and monument to her: the Parthenon. It still stands today, reminding everyone who sees it of their love for Athena.

review of evidence

reminder of opening question

THE END!

29

opinion or evidence?

When you write a research report, you use **evidence**— or facts—to support your opinions. In each pair below, can you tell which statement is evidence and which is opinion?

In Greek mythology, Athena was the goddess of wisdom, war, and solving conflicts with reason.

Athena is the most interesting Greek god because she represented war and peace at the same time.

Rabbits make the best pets for people who live in apartments because they are quiet and they can be trained to use a litter box.

Rabbits are quiet pets that can be trained to use a litter box.

1.

2.

3.

The government of the United States is made up of three branches: the legislative, the judicial, and the executive.

The judicial branch of our federal government is less important in making laws than the legislative branch or the executive branch.

4.

Grand Canyon National Park is the most beautiful place in America.

Grand Canyon National Park is known the world over for its beauty.

5.

Meriwether Lewis's discoveries in the Louisiana Territory are the most significant ever made by an American explorer.

Meriwether Lewis explored the land acquired by the United States in the Louisiana Purchase and kept detailed records of what he discovered there.

answers

The statements in **green** are **facts.** That makes them evidence. The **blue** statements are **opinions.** Each opinion statement is a judgment, belief, or feeling that is based on facts but is not a fact itself. Words like *best, worst, important,* and *beautiful* signal that a statement is opinion. Your opinions are what make a report your own, and your audience wants to know what you think, so do include them! Just be sure to support them with evidence in any research project.

POSTERS THAT POP

Communicate your message at a glance with a great poster.

Posters can instantly capture your audience's attention and draw them into your topic. The purpose of a poster is to give an overview of your ideas. You don't need to include every fascinating fact you've discovered—save those details for your report or speech.

Get ready to glue with these steps:

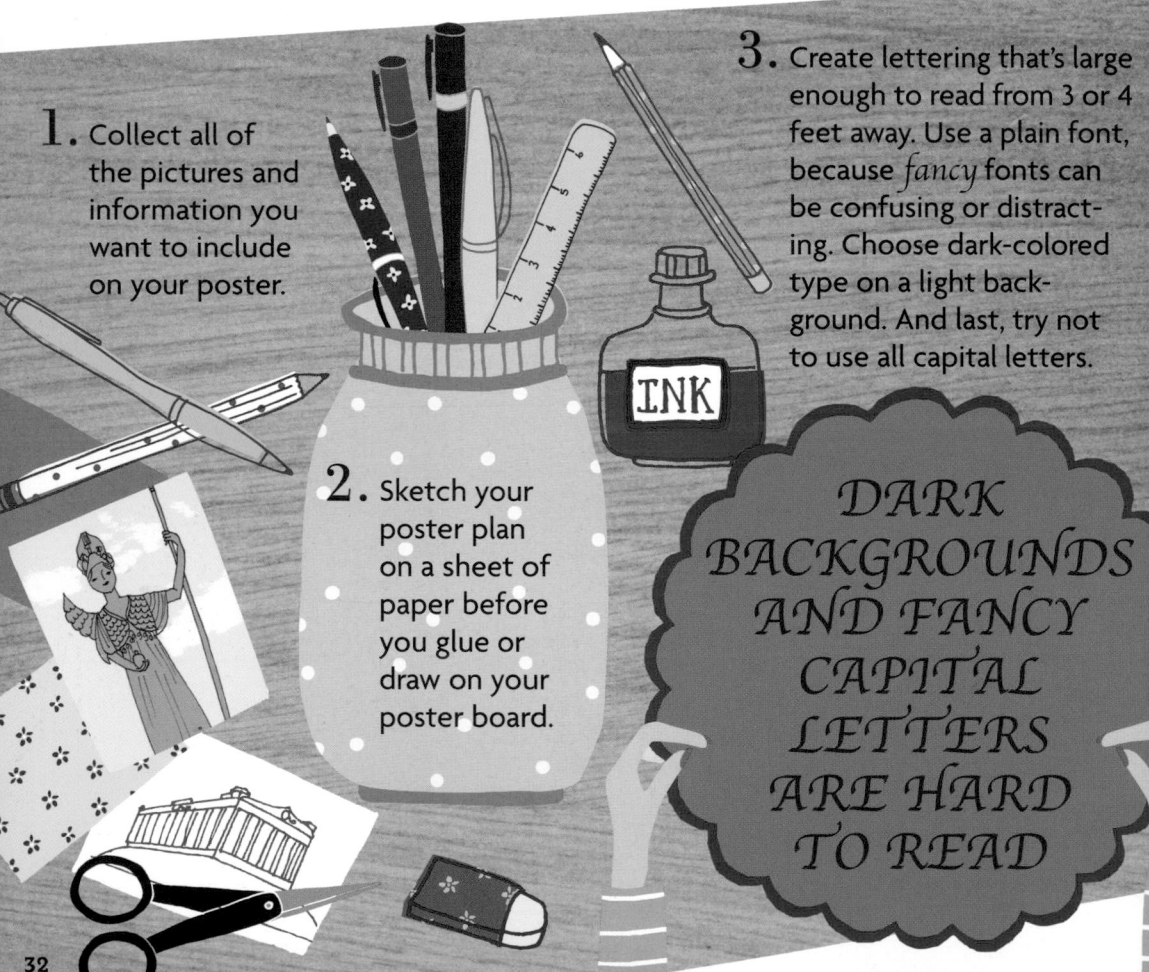

1. Collect all of the pictures and information you want to include on your poster.

2. Sketch your poster plan on a sheet of paper before you glue or draw on your poster board.

3. Create lettering that's large enough to read from 3 or 4 feet away. Use a plain font, because *fancy* fonts can be confusing or distracting. Choose dark-colored type on a light background. And last, try not to use all capital letters.

INK

DARK BACKGROUNDS AND FANCY CAPITAL LETTERS ARE HARD TO READ

Have faces look straight ahead or toward the middle of the poster instead of the edge.

Your poster title should have a big, bold font.

Athena and Athens

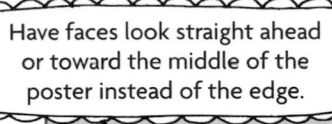

Why was the goddess of wisdom and war so important to the people of ancient Athens?

- She was the city's patron goddess and gave the people helpful gifts.
- Athens was the intellectual center of ancient Greece.
- She stood for justice and reason, even in war.

Don't crowd the poster with too many images or too much text.

According to mythology, Athena became the goddess of Athens because of her gift of the olive tree. She planted the tree on the Acropolis, which was the ancient hill where Athenians built the Parthenon (right) to honor her.

Try to give the same amount of space to text as you do to images.

Use dark letters in a plain font against a light background so the words are easy to read.

Use two or three colors— not the whole rainbow.

TOOLS OF THE TRADE

Add polish to your poster with the right equipment.

POSTER BOARD BASICS

Use a sturdy poster board that can stand on its own. A poster that flops over halfway through your presentation distracts from your ideas. If you need a large area for your information, use a trifold poster board. Add support to a flimsy poster board by gluing thick cardboard to the back.

WAYS WITH WORDS

Use a computer and printer to create text for your poster. Your text will be consistent, neat, and easy to read. Not sure how large to make your letters? Follow the guidelines on the next page.

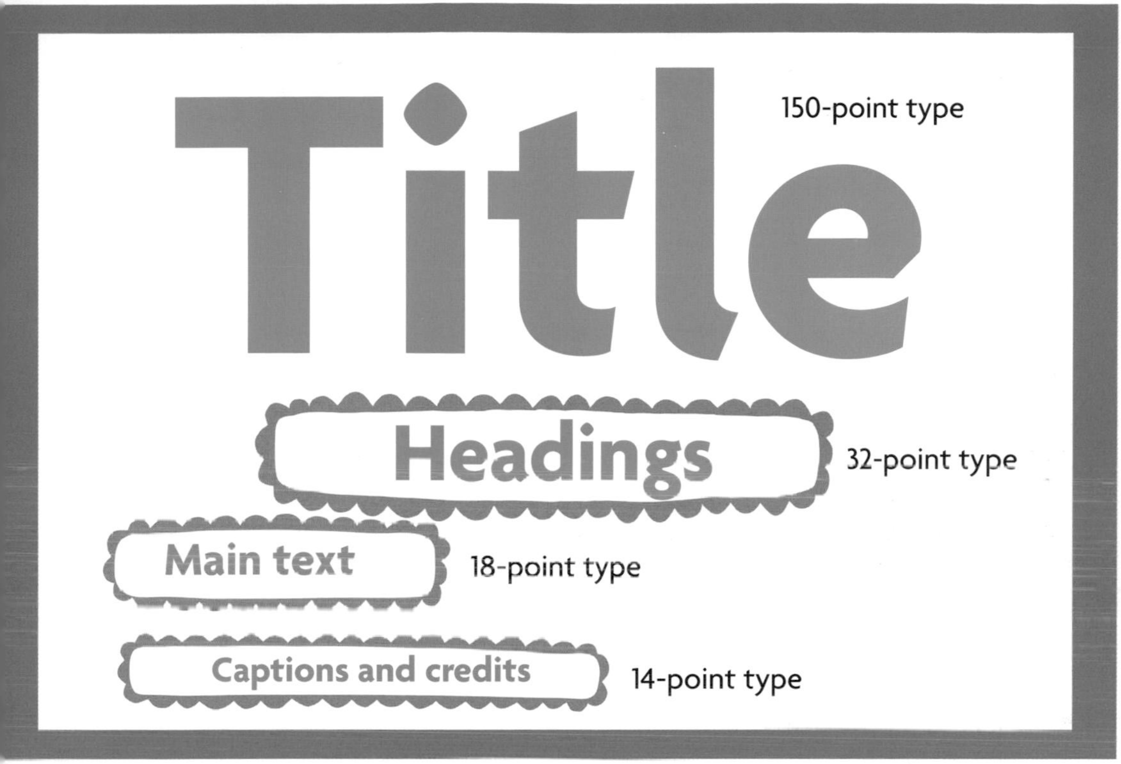

Title
150-point type
Headings
32-point type
Main text
18-point type
Captions and credits
14-point type

Outstanding Colors

Place your printed text on colored construction paper backgrounds. This helps your text stand out, especially if you're using a white poster board.

Exacting Edges

Ask your parents for help cutting out photos, pictures, and text with a straight edge and utility knife. Or use a straight edge and pencil to draw cutting guidelines around images and text, and use scissors to cut along the guidelines. Straight, even cuts make your poster look sharp!

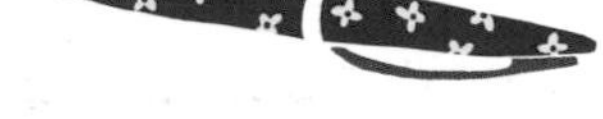

Flat Attachments

Firmly attach text and images to your poster board with a glue stick or double-sided tape. Avoid liquid glue, because it can make your paper warp and wrinkle.

0 1 2 3 4 5 6 7 8 9 10 11 12

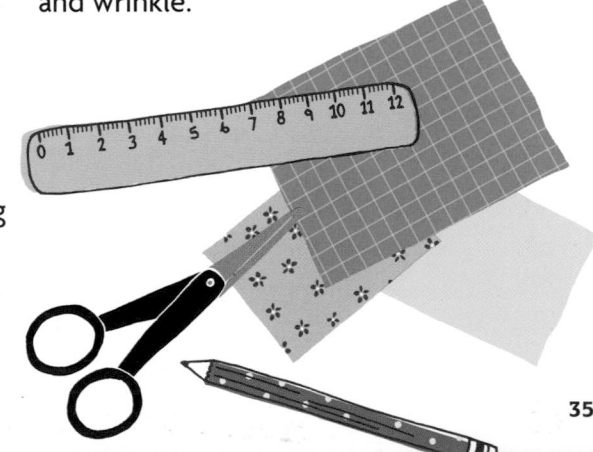

POSTER PERFECT?

Not every project idea makes a powerful poster. Choose the project in each pair that could be turned into the more successful poster.

1. a. information about family life in ancient Greece

b. a family tree of ancient Greek gods and goddesses

2. a. how to fold a basic paper airplane

b. how to fold an origami crane

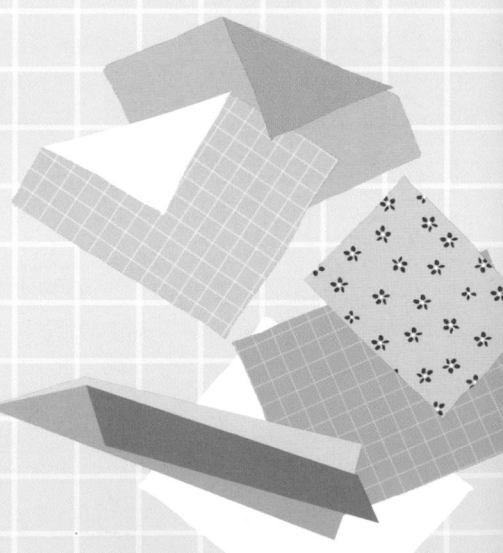

3. a. the history of your family name

b. the countries where your ancestors lived

4. a. an interpretation of a Shakespeare sonnet

b. a diagram of Shakespeare's Globe Theatre

5. a. the meaning of the parts of the American flag

b. the meaning of the words in the national anthem

answers

The best topics for posters have a strong but simple visual element. That means you can clearly "see" a few pictures in your imagination. Some ideas, like the meaning of a poem or song, are easier to explore with words than images, so a paper or speech is a better choice. And some ideas, even if they are visual, are too complicated or require too many steps to show in a poster. For those ideas, plan a demonstration instead.

1. b; 2. a; 3. b; 4. b; 5. a

super speeches

Follow a few script-writing secrets for a polished performance of any oral report.

Every great speech begins with great writing. Plan and research an oral report just like you would a written version, and then craft a draft that includes . . .

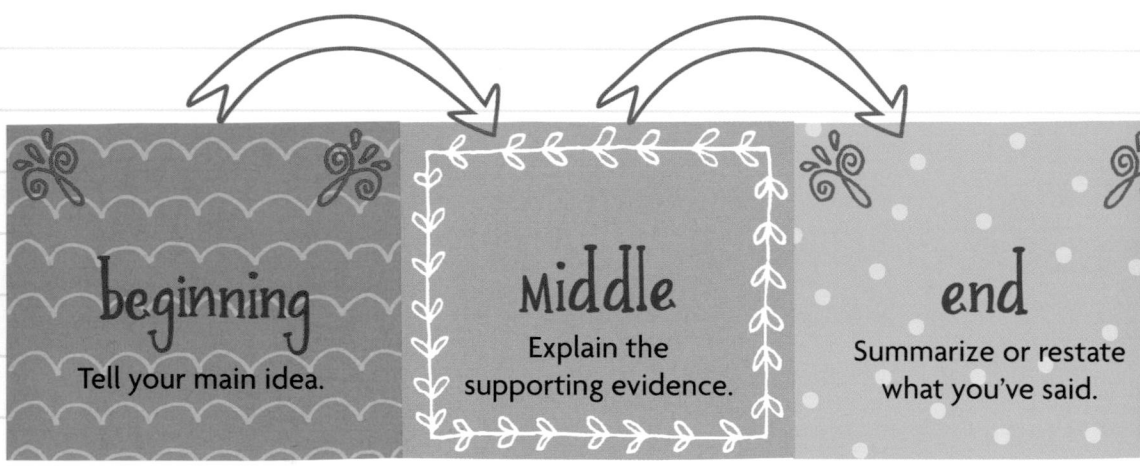

beginning
Tell your main idea.

Middle
Explain the supporting evidence.

end
Summarize or restate what you've said.

Begin your speech with an attention-getter. You might . . .

tell a story

According to mythology, Athena became the goddess of Athens in a contest . . .

use humor

Athena wasn't born in the regular way. She burst from Zeus's head! Ouch!

ask a question

Picture the Parthenon! Did you know it's a temple to the goddess Athena?

You could also start with a surprising fact, or share a quote, or come up with your own attention-grabbing idea.

SHOW AND TELL

With an oral report, you can *show* while you tell. If you have props, a costume, a demonstration, or other visual aids that make your report more interesting or your ideas easier to share, ask your teacher if you can use them. They can help you communicate. Plus, having something to do or to hold can help calm any jitters you might be feeling!

TALKING TIP

Use conversational language when you write a speech. Write it the way you would naturally say it.

WRAPPING UP

Just like you do in a written report, end your speech with a summary of your ideas. Then leave your audience with a question or quote to ponder— or with a good laugh!

Practice makes a performance

You've finished writing your report. Now what?

You could call it done and just stand in front of the class, reading straight from your paper. But that's not a true oral report. It's probably not what your teacher is expecting, and it's kind of boring for the audience. How can you make it a speech—or even a performance?

Card Tricks

With note cards—*presto!*—a written report is transformed into a speech. Read through your draft, picking out the big ideas and transferring them to cards, one idea per card.

Don't include every word from your report—write only enough to help you remember each point you want to make. Why? Jotting notes or bullet points instead of copying word-for-word helps you *speak* your speech instead of just reading it. It frees you to talk to your audience and connect with your eyes, your face, your voice, and your gestures.

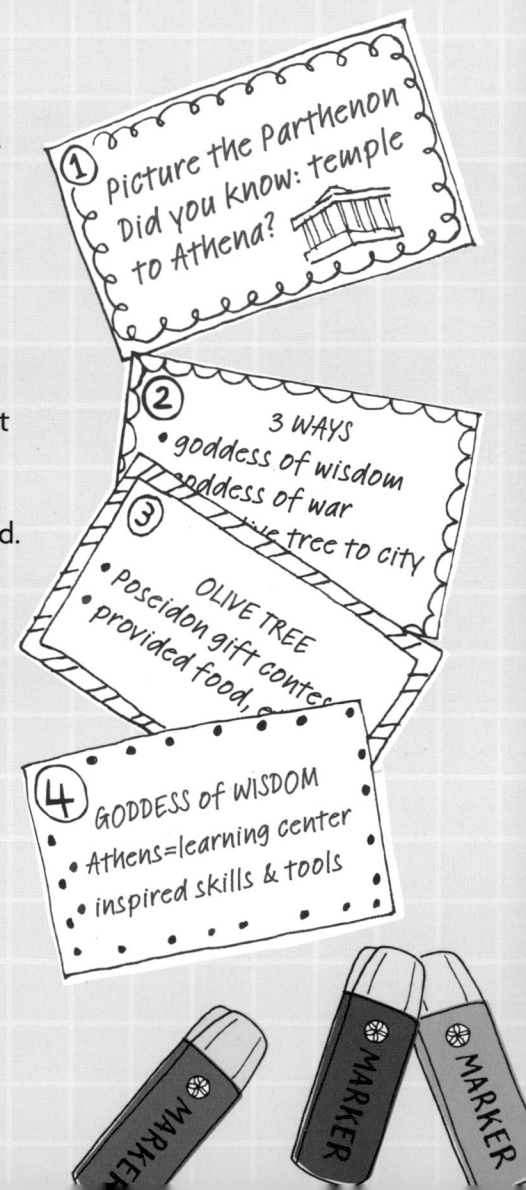

① Picture the Parthenon
Did you know: temple to Athena?

② 3 WAYS
• goddess of wisdom
• goddess of war
• gave tree to city

③ OLIVE TREE
• Poseidon gift contest
• provided food,

④ GODDESS of WISDOM
• Athens=learning center
• inspired skills & tools

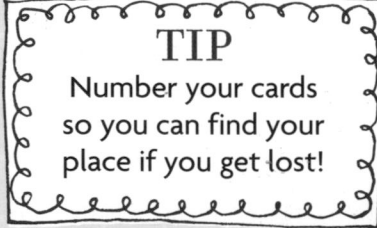

TIP
Number your cards so you can find your place if you get lost!

Rehearse

With your note cards, practice your speech by yourself in front of a mirror or an audience of stuffed animals. Then, when you're ready, you can try it in front of your parents, siblings, or friends. Each time you run through your speech, see if you can rely on your cards a little less. You don't have to say it the exact same way each time!

Showtime

Remembering a few simple tips when you're in front of the room will help you deliver a *class* performance.

Breathe! Take a nice deep one.

Speak slower and louder than you think you should. People often talk too fast and quietly when they're in the spotlight. You want your audience to hear you!

Smile.
Look a friend or two in the eye.

Tell yourself, "I like my topic, and I know a lot!" If you're enthusiastic, your audience will be, too.

catch your confidence

Would nerves stop you from giving a star performance?
Choose the answers that sound most like you.

1. As you write your speech, you're likely to tell yourself . . .

   a. "I have no idea what to say. Even though I've done the research, I just can't come up with the words. I might as well wing it at speech time."

   b. "I've researched my topic thoroughly, so writing a few words to share will be a breeze."

2. The night before it's due, you . . .

   a. can't sleep at all. You know you're going to blow it.

   b. rest easy. You've prepped and practiced, and you understand your topic well.

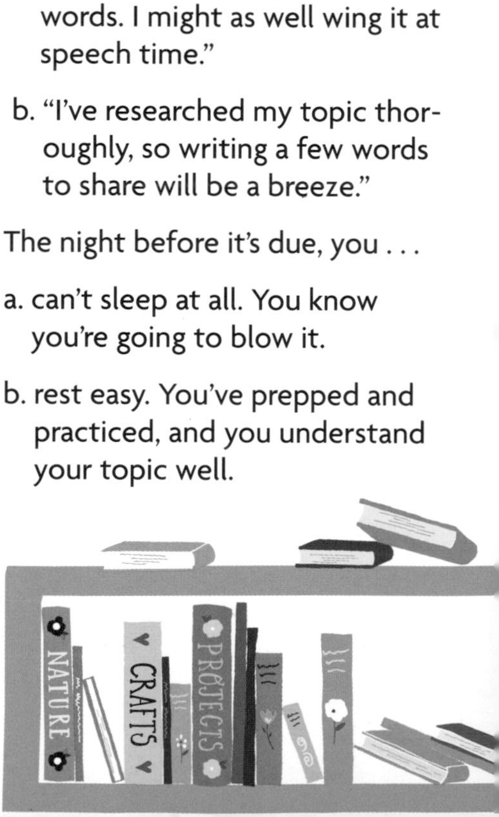

3. It's a few minutes before you give your speech, and excitement has your mouth feeling dry. You decide to . . .

   a. skip a sip of water, for sure! What if you have to go to the bathroom right in the middle of your speech?

   b. get a quick drink. Water will help you stay cool and keep your voice flowing.

4. As you step in front of the class, you're . . .

   a. too terrified to breathe!

   b. breathing deeply to calm any last-minute jitters.

5. In the middle of your presentation, you stumble over a couple of words. You . . .

   a. start speaking as quickly as you can to get this speech over with!

   b. pause briefly, then pick up where you left off. Everyone misspeaks from time to time.

6. When you reach the end, you . . .

   a. wipe your hand across your forehead with a sigh of relief as you mumble, "At least that's over with."

   b. pause, give your audience a confident smile, and return to your seat, happy that you did your best.

Answers

If you picked mostly **b's,** congrats! You're one cool cucumber. But if you chose a lot of **a's,** don't fret. Speaking in front of others makes many people—even adults—feel nervous. The best way to tame your worries is simple: Just practice as much as you can. Start without an audience, then work up to performing for your family or close friends. You could even try recording your practice sessions. Watch, listen, and decide if you need to speak louder, more slowly, or with more emotion. When speech time comes, if you've practiced, you'll feel more relaxed than you ever thought you could!

Brainy Book Reports

What's the first step toward a successful book report?
Finding a good book!

Your teacher might provide a list of books, or she might tell you to read one by a certain author or from a particular **genre,** such as biography, historical fiction, or fantasy. Follow the instructions in your book report assignment. If the instructions are more open-ended, let your interests guide you to a great read.

You can look for a book on the **Internet.** Library websites, book review websites, and bookseller websites all give suggestions based on books you like.

Look for books at your **reading level** that interest you the most. The more you both like and understand a book, the better you'll be able to write about it.

If you're not sure where to begin, ask a **librarian** for help. Librarians specialize in helping you find just-right, report-ready books.

Think about how long you have. Is there **enough time** to read that 397-page book and write your report?

DON'T FORGET TO CHECK OUT . . .

AWARD-WINNING BOOKS
Winners of the Newbery, Coretta Scott King, and other awards also make winning book reports.

BIOGRAPHIES AND MEMOIRS
Get to know heroes, historical figures, and other famous people.

HISTORY
Take a deep dive into your favorite time period or event.

GRAPHIC NOVELS
Illustrations help tell complex stories in these much-more-than-comic books.

INVESTIGATIVE NONFICTION
Learn the secrets behind news stories, successful businesses, the government, and more.

INSTRUCTIVE NONFICTION
Learn a new skill through reading.

CLOSE READING

Take notes as you read your book. Keep track of characters, plotlines, and big ideas. Write in a notebook, and use sticky notes to flag pages inside the book. Copy quotes you love or that reveal important themes. If you can, include a quote or two in your report.

 ## ⚠ WARNING

Read the book. Sure, book summaries are easy to find online. But your teacher will probably know you didn't read the book. And *you* will definitely know.

REPORT RIGHT

When you're ready to draft your report, include this important information. If you write a paragraph for each point, you'll end up with a solid report.

title & author

What is your book called? Who wrote it? Has the author written other noteworthy books?

main action

For fiction, what is the plot of the book? For nonfiction, what is the book about? Even nonfiction books tell a story. What is that story?

genre

Is the book realistic fiction, historical fiction, biography, fantasy, mystery, a fairy tale? Explain how your book fits into its genre.

SPOILER ALERT Consider your audience when you decide whether to reveal the book's ending. If you're sharing your report with classmates, you might want to save the surprises for them to discover on their own.

people

Who is the book about? For fiction, does the book have one central character? For nonfiction, is a person the book's subject? If not, how are people involved with the subject?

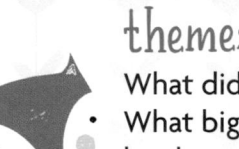

themes

What did you learn from the book? What big idea does the book communicate?

your recommendation

Did you love the book? Hate it? Or did it leave you feeling bored? Give your opinion, and tell if you'd recommend the book to other readers.

NOVEL IDEAS

Tired of basic book reviews? Try one of these fun formats for your next report.

Create an **advertisement** for the book. Illustrate a scene that will sell the story to other readers and highlight the book's best point.

Get **in character.** Dress up like the hero or protagonist of the book and present your report as her or him.

Create your own **comic book** version of the book you read.

Design your own **book jacket,** including the front-cover illustration and a book description and celebrity reviews on the back and the flaps.

Demonstrate a **skill** you learned from the book.

Make up a **board game** based on the book. Ask trivia questions. Label game squares with situations from your story: "Charlotte spins a web for you. Move ahead 4 spaces."

Collect objects that appear in the book, and use them as **props** in a speech about the main events.

Write and perform a **skit** based on a favorite scene.

Memorize and perform a **speech** made by one of the characters.

CReaTIVe CRaFTS

These tips will help you show what you know with a model, diorama, or another craft project.

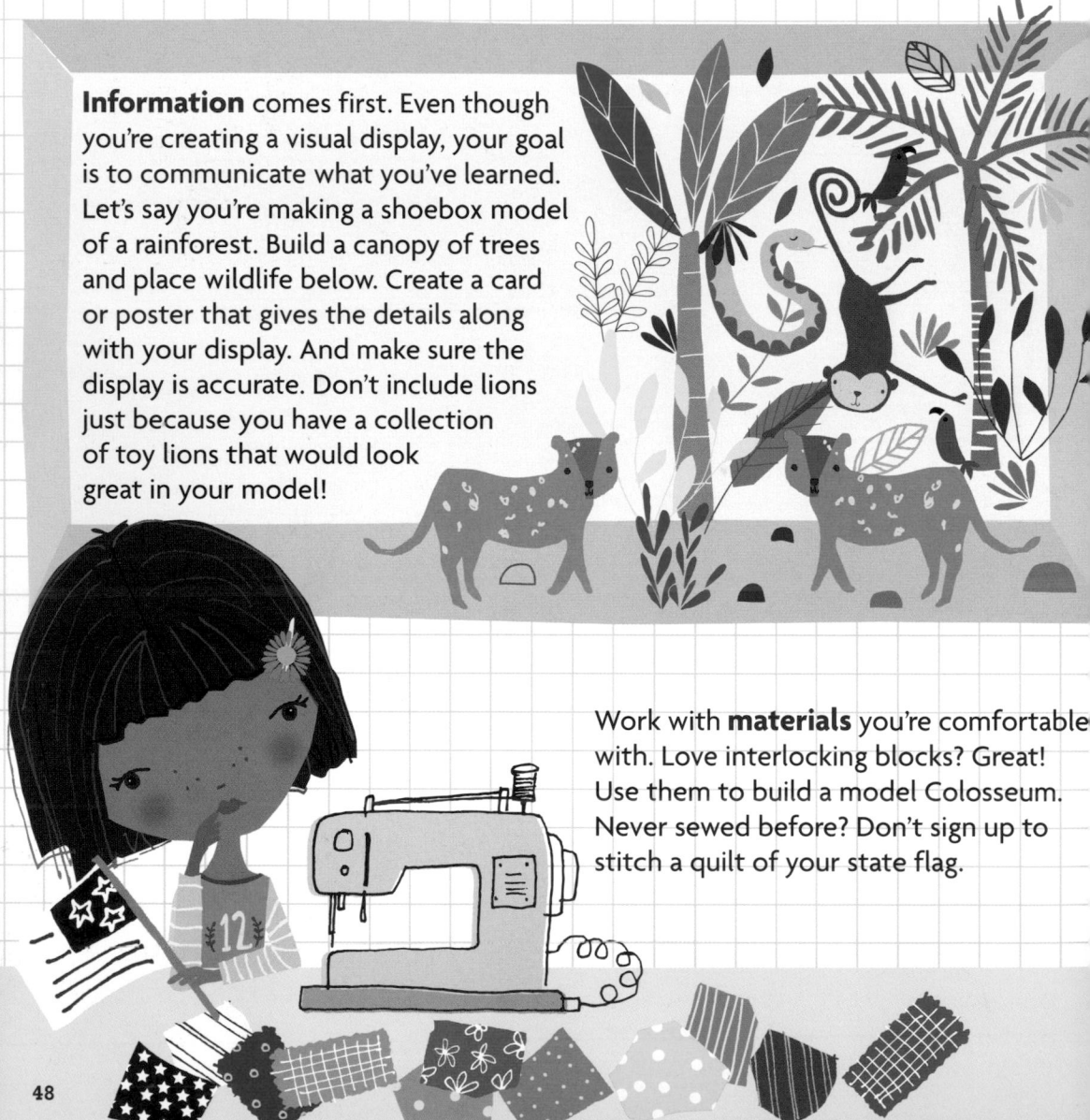

Information comes first. Even though you're creating a visual display, your goal is to communicate what you've learned. Let's say you're making a shoebox model of a rainforest. Build a canopy of trees and place wildlife below. Create a card or poster that gives the details along with your display. And make sure the display is accurate. Don't include lions just because you have a collection of toy lions that would look great in your model!

Work with **materials** you're comfortable with. Love interlocking blocks? Great! Use them to build a model Colosseum. Never sewed before? Don't sign up to stitch a quilt of your state flag.

Keep **scale** in mind. When you plan the size of your model or display, remember you'll need to collect or buy all the supplies. Plus, you've got to be able to carry it to school!

Make sure your project isn't too **fragile,** especially if it will be on display at school. A tippy toothpick model of the Eiffel Tower will tumble down with the slightest bump!

Pay attention to **details.** Take your time and do neat work. Cut carefully. Draw in pencil before you use markers or paint. Let paint and glue dry completely before you move on to the next step.

Give proper **credit.** On a small card that you display with your project, list the sources for the information and images you used to create it.

SOURCES

Information
Paul Probst. Life in the Rainforest
Osborn Press, 2012
B. Stretchberry. Wild Animals
Sam & Me Books, 2004
Pictures
National Diorama Magazine,
June 2017

CRAFT BLAST!

Move beyond models with these clever craft projects.

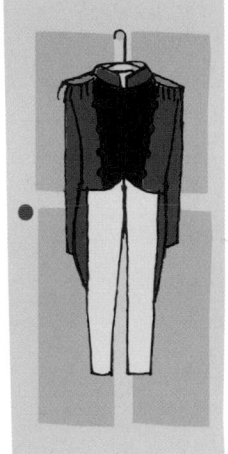

Make a **costume.** Show how a historical figure or book character might dress. Use clothing you have or old Halloween costumes. Or cut and tape tissue paper and construction paper into a one-time-wear display.

Make a **mobile.** Imagine a hanging solar system or anatomy display.

Craft **puppets** for your own puppet show. Act out a scene from history or your book report book.

Design a **board game.** Create the board with labeled game squares, make cards, and craft game tokens that reflect your subject.

Lay out a **photo collage.** Use photos you take yourself, printouts from the Internet, or photocopies from books.

Create a **museum exhibit.** Imagine you're the curator of a museum show on the subject you researched. What would you show? What information would you share?

LIFE IN THE MIDDLE AGES
FOOD: CLOTHES:
                    JOBS:

HOMES: ART:

Fold a **cootie catcher** filled with trivia questions and answers about your research subject.

GET TECHY

Use your computer to bring projects to life!

Computers let you combine words, images, sounds, and even movies to share what you have learned. With digital presentations, your audience can even interact with the info you gathered.

One tech project your teacher may assign is a digital **slide show.** With a slide show program, you fill a series of slides with words and pictures. If you want, you can also add sounds and short movies.

Before you create a slide show, answer these all-important questions:

? Will you actually present the information to the class, talking them through your slides?

(OR)

? Will your audience view the slides on their own, using a computer to see your work?

If you're talking your audience through your slides, think of them as digital note cards that you'll share. If your presentation will stand alone, make sure everyone can see your main ideas without help.

super slides

Follow these tips for putting together a perfect presentation.

Organize Your Info

Organize the information just like you do with a research report:

- Introduction: Tell your audience what you're going to say.
- Body: Say it.
- Conclusion: Tell them what you said.

Word Count

- Present only one idea per slide so you don't load slides with too many words.
- Aim for 30 words or fewer in each slide.
- Use bullet points to help you lower the word count.
- Exception: If you use quotes, it's okay to use more words.

Design Basics

- Choose a slide template that's not too busy or informal for a school project.
- Add images such as photos, art, and videos. Reporting on red pandas? Show what they look like!
- Design each slide like a mini-poster. See the layout tips on pages 32-33.

Charts, Graphs, and Maps

Show your data as well as telling about it.

- Comparing students' favorite school lunches? Show a pie chart.
- For your red panda report? Use a map to show where in the world they live.

Media Matters

Any image or video you put on a slide should support the idea or information on that slide.

Q: In which report can you use that adorable movie you found of a lion cub taking its first steps?
   a. "The Rocks of the Grand Canyon"
   b. "How to Play a Trombone"
   c. "Baby Animals in the Wild"   Answer: c

Showtime?

- If you're presenting your slide show to the class, prepare just like you would to give a speech.
- Use your slides like your note cards.
- Review the practice and presentation tips on pages 38-41.

Red Pandas

- ♥ endangered species
- ♥ in the raccoon family
- ♥ eat bamboo like giant pandas

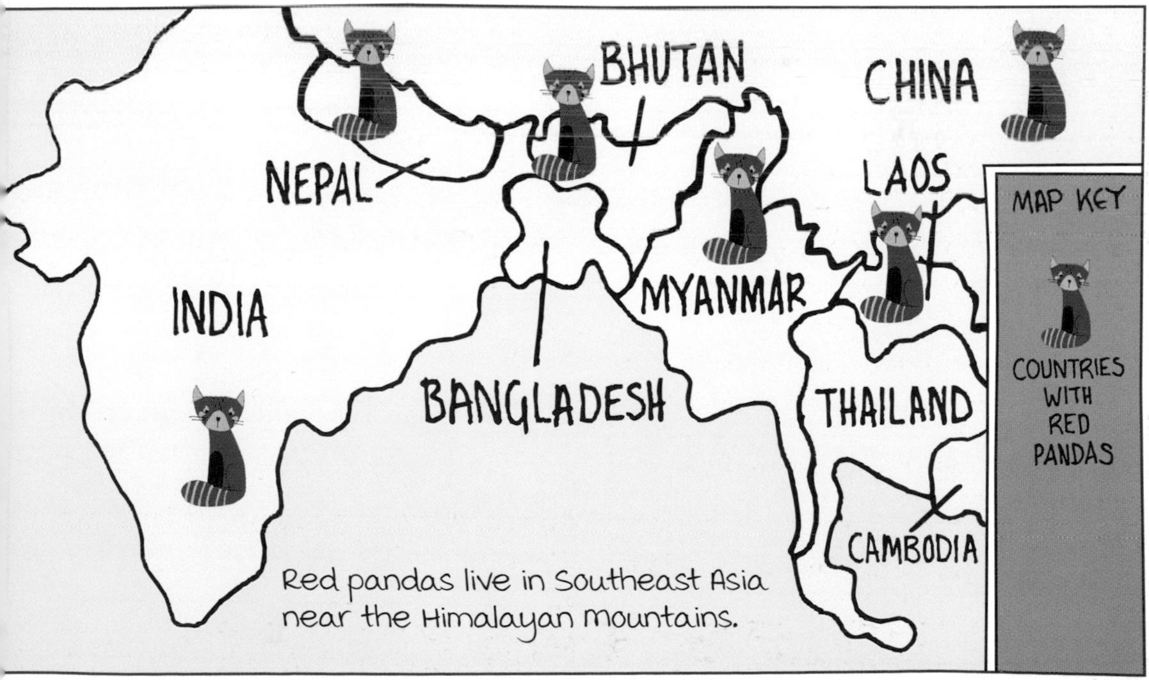

NEPAL

BHUTAN

CHINA

INDIA

LAOS

MYANMAR

BANGLADESH

THAILAND

CAMBODIA

Red pandas live in Southeast Asia near the Himalayan mountains.

MAP KEY

COUNTRIES WITH RED PANDAS

TROUBLESHOOT YOUR TECH

With a little advance prep, you can make sure your presentation will run as smoothly as possible.

Before the due date, run your presentation at least three times to make sure it works the way you want it to. Do your slides look the way you thought? Do sounds and videos play as planned? Do your slides change without getting stuck?

Plan how you'll access your project at school. Will you create your project at home and bring it to school on a thumb drive? Will you e-mail it to your teacher? Will you create your project with a web-based program that stores it online so you can get to it from any computer? In any case, make sure your project plays the same on your school computer as it does at home.

If possible, test your project at school the day before you present it.

If you do run into tech trouble, ask your teacher, school librarian, or another adult for help with figuring out what to do.

DIGITAL DOMAIN

Are you looking for more ways to polish your projects with technology? With the right program, you can . . .

create a talking photo with online software that helps you digitally animate a photo or drawing. For a project on Amelia Earhart, for example, you can make the famous flyer speak the words of your report.

record your own narration for a photo slide show.

film and edit your own movie.

use online programming software to create a trivia game or digital jigsaw puzzle.

If you're not sure where to start, ask a tech-smart adult for help finding online software and programs.

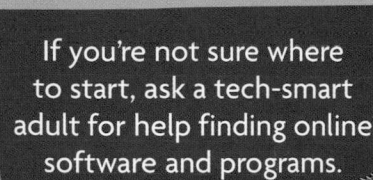

science Fair Flair

Experiment your way to science fair success!

Science fair projects call for a different approach than other kinds of research projects. Instead of reporting on information from sources like encyclopedias and websites, you design and conduct an experiment to create your own information—*your own evidence*—in the form of experiment results.

To do this, you use something called the **scientific method.** First you decide on a question that you want to answer with your experiment. Then you form a **hypothesis**—a good guess about the answer to your question or what your experiment will show. Finally, you test your hypothesis with the experiment.

Six Steps to Science Fair Success

1. Ask a question.

Come up with a science question that interests you and that you can answer with an experiment. Think about questions from your everyday life:

Which brand of battery lasts the longest?

Can young people hear higher-pitched sounds than older people?

How can you keep fruit fresh in the fridge the longest?

Or use an idea from your school science class:

What's the best kind of light to grow seedlings?

What freezes faster: plain water, salt water, or sugar water?

Talk to your science teacher and check the Internet for more question and experiment ideas.

2. Do background research on your topic.

Suppose you choose this question:

What brand of battery lasts the longest?

You might visit the hardware store or check online to see which brands of batteries cost the most and the least.

When you're looking at brands of batteries, you might find other differences that you'll want to talk about in your experiment, such as the size of the battery and whether it's alkaline. You want to be sure you're comparing apples with apples—or AA batteries with AA batteries!

You might check consumer magazines to see if your question has been studied.

3. Form a hypothesis.

A **hypothesis** is your best guess about the answer to your question or what you think will happen. Use your background research and common sense to come up with your hypothesis:

I think the expensive battery Lightlife will outlast the midprice brand Strongcell and the bargain brand SuperPower when tested in a flashlight.

4. Design and conduct your experiment.

When you plan your experiment, make sure you can get it done in the time you have, and that you have everything you need to do it. Does your experiment need a microscope? If so, is there one you can use at school or home? Do you want to survey 100 kids who are all 10 years old? If so, can you find that many?

If you're testing batteries, your experiment plan might look something like this:

Time how long two AA alkaline batteries from three different brands (expensive brand, medium-price brand, and bargain brand) will power three identical flashlights that are left on continuously.

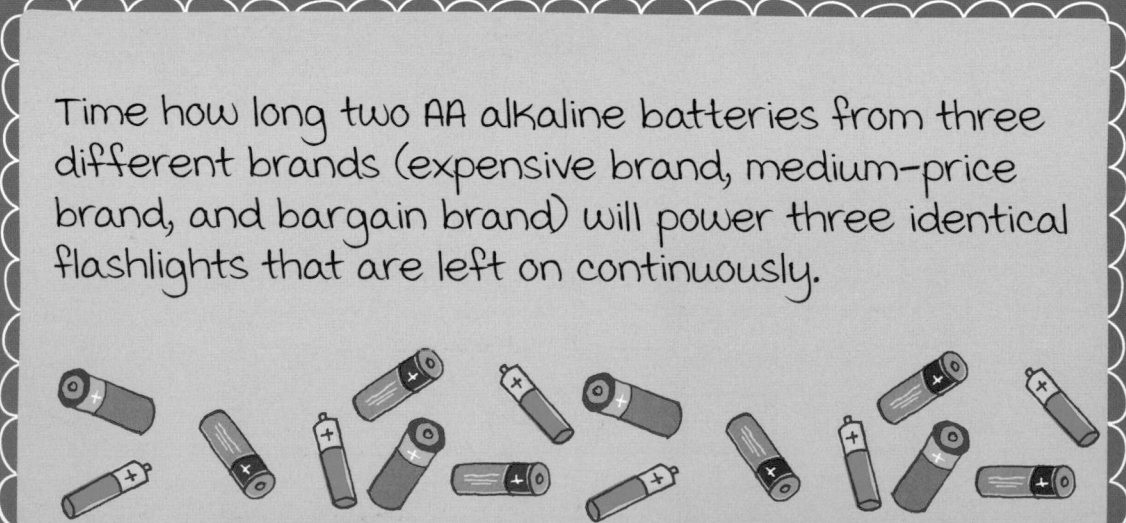

For this experiment, you might want to choose a flashlight (or other device or toy) that you know drains batteries quickly!

Make sure you carefully record your results as you conduct your experiment.

BATTERY BRAND	Time Until Battery Ran Out		
	TEST 1	TEST 2	TEST 3
Bargain	6:02	5:56	5:49
Medium price	4:30	4:38	4:33
Expensive	4:56	4:53	4:57

5. Review your results and draw your conclusion.

Take a look at your results. How do they compare to your hypothesis? In other words, do your results support your hypothesis, or do they lead you to a different conclusion? Maybe you discovered that in your test, the bargain brand batteries actually lasted the longest!

BIG IDEA

Science fair projects are not about knowing the answer ahead of time. They're about reporting and reflecting on **what you actually discover** through a science experiment. Results that do not support your hypothesis are as good—and as important to science—as results that do support it! In the scientific method, it's all about the process.

6. Present your experiment.

Create a poster or display to share your results at the science fair. Make sure to include . . .

1 **a title!** A good title tells people right away what your experiment is about.

2 **your question.** What did you want to find out?

3 **your hypothesis.** What was your best guess—the answer you thought you might get to your question?

4 **your background research.** Summarize what you discovered before you started your experiment.

5 **a description of your experiment.** Using step-by-step directions, give a written explanation of what you did to test your hypothesis.

6 **photos or drawings of the experiment.** Include images to make your poster both more interesting and more informative.

7 **a list of materials used.** Be very specific, including such details as sizes, brand names, and other identifying information.

8 **a written summary of your results.** Results are facts, or *data*. For example, in Results you would tell how long each battery lasted and which battery lasted the longest and the shortest.

9 **a chart or graph to show the results.** Give it a title that explains the data, and make sure the elements are identified clearly.

10 **a conclusion.** What did you learn? What lesson can you draw from your results? Is there anything you would do differently next time? If the least expensive battery lasted the longest (your results), you could conclude that the price of a battery does not indicate how long it will last.

presentation pointers

Follow any directions from your teacher on the requirements for your science fair poster.

Use a trifold display board (available at most office supply stores) so that your project stands on its own.

Print out the text that will appear on your display instead of writing it by hand.

Follow the other poster layout tips on pages 32–35.

Which Battery _____ _____ ?

① Which Battery _____ ?

Results ⑧

② **Question**
Which brand of _____
_____
_____

③ **Hypothesis**
I think the expensive _____
_____
_____

④ **Background Research**

⑤ **Experiment**

⑩ **Conclusion**

⑥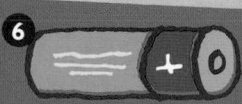

⑦ **Materials**

⑨ How Long Did It Light?

Time
6
5
4
3
2
1
0

STRONGCELL | SUPERPOWER | LIGHTLIFE

Battery Brand

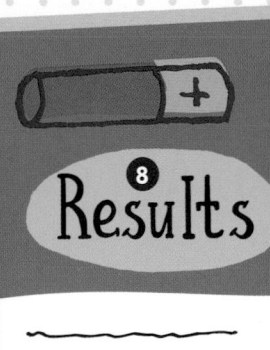
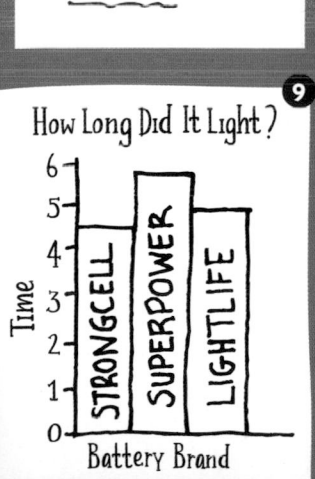

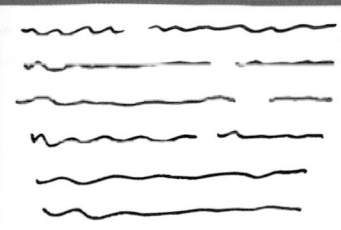

lend a Hand

Make the most of your school service project!

School service projects are all about making a difference in your community. When you support a cause or help people in need, you get a larger view of the world. You gain organizational skills and experience working as part of a team. And it feels good to know you're making the world a better place.

Choose the right project.

Your teacher or school may set up your service project and assign your part in it. But sometimes you get to choose a project or even create your own.

If the choice is yours, try relating your project to something you love or that you're learning in school. Studying wildlife in your area? Volunteer to help at a local nature preserve. Working on some special songs with your school choir? Set up a time to sing for the residents of a nearby nursing home. Breezing through math class? See if you can help tutor younger students.

Be realistic about what you can accomplish and about your time. If you're creating your own project, it's easy to take on too much. Check with your teacher and your parents to make sure your idea is manageable.

ASK FOR ADULT HELP.

Service projects are one kind of assignment that teachers do *not* expect you to do on your own! Be safe and smart. Ask your parents or teacher to help you contact organizations you'd like to help and decide on the role that's right for you.

MAKE A COMMITMENT.

When you sign up for a service project, keep in mind that others are counting on you. If you say you'll help stock shelves at the local food pantry once a month, be there as agreed, doing your part.

HOW can YOU HeLP?

Wondering what kind of volunteer project is the best fit for you? Take this quiz to find out.

1. To help out with All-School Clean-Up Day, you'd . . .

   a. make posters to spread the word.
   b. pitch in with dusting and vacuuming. You've got lots of experience from home.
   c. teach younger kids how to weed the school's vegetable garden.

2. Your class decides to volunteer at a local food pantry. You'd sign up to . . .

   a. stock shelves.
   b. help teach a kids' cooking class in the food pantry's kitchen.
   c. organize a food drive at school.

3. You and your classmates want to start a "book buddies" program at your school that pairs older students with beginning readers to share library favorites. You'd . . .

   a. lead a book circle with the kindergarten class.
   b. volunteer to partner with a younger reading pal.
   c. match volunteers with younger buddies.

4. To finish your science unit on circulation and the heart, your class will take part in a walk-a-thon to raise money for heart disease research. You decide to . . .

   a. distribute water to thirsty walkers.
   b. make a flyer showing how walking improves heart health to pass out on the big day.
   c. talk to all your relatives, friends, and neighbors and ask for pledges.

5. Your English class has decided to create a school news magazine. You'd volunteer to . . .

a. take pictures. You're pretty good with a camera.
b. be a reporter. You'd love to share the scoop at school.
c. be the editor! You'll keep the whole magazine on track.

answers

Did you choose several **blues?** You might succeed in a job that makes the most of your organizing skills. Use your talents to help raise money and awareness for a good cause. You'd make a good leader for any student-driven service project.

Did you pick mostly **purples?** You'd probably enjoy pitching in with the action on any project, especially if you can use your experience. Check with the volunteer coordinator for a cause or project you believe in to find the hands-on role that's right for you.

Did you select **violet** answers most? You're a natural teacher! You'd likely thrive in a service project that lets you share what you know. Perhaps you can tutor younger students at school, or volunteer to help with another group where you can teach new skills.

Information, PLEASE!

Find and manage the facts you need for a top-notch project.

GET READY TO RESEARCH

What's one essential ingredient in the recipe for any great school project? Information!

Information is everywhere: books, newspapers, magazines, the Internet, TV. With so much info out there—*too* much, in fact—how can you find just what you need? And how can you sort smart sources from the less-than-the-best? Here's how to research right.

WHEN? WHY? WHO?

HOW? WHERE? WHAT?

You've already decided on your topic. The first step in doing your research is writing questions that will guide your search. Start by asking the basics: Who? What? When? Where? Why? and How?

Come up with specific questions by listing everything you already know about your topic—and what you'd like to find out.

Topic	What do I know?	What do I want to find out?
Eiffel Tower	• in Paris, France • top tourist site • made of metal • has restaurant inside	• Who designed it? Who built it? • When was it built? • Why was it built? • What are some other interesting facts or stories about the Eiffel Tower?

research needs

Different kinds of projects require different kinds of information.

❀ For a report, you'll need facts.

❀ For a service project, you'll need information about the groups you might help or the causes you want to support.

❀ For a biography project, you'll need information about the person's life, plus pictures or photos and maybe even props.

Once you have some ideas about what you want to find out, you can begin your research.

Love your Library

Think of your library as Information Central,
and head there to start your search.

BOOKS

Books are a great place to begin, and they have certain features that can help you find the facts you need fast.

Index Start at the back of the book! Turn to the index and look up your topic. Then scan the pages listed in the index for information you can use.

Contents Read the table of contents to find chapters that may relate to your topic. Then skim the chapters that look helpful, paying attention to titles and headings. Read carefully when you find info directly linked to your topic.

Visuals Flip through chapters that touch on your topic, looking for charts, graphs, or photos you can use.

Library catalog number Did you find a useful book? Visit the spot on the library shelf where you discovered it. Nonfiction books in the library are shelved according to their cataloging number, which means that books about the same subject have the same number and are grouped together.

BIG IDEA

Whatever subject you're researching, ask the **librarian** for help! She or he knows exactly how to find the very best books, magazines, reference materials, and online information for your project.

Magazines and Newspapers

Check out periodicals—publications like magazines that come out *periodically*, such as every day, week, or month. Current issues are on the shelves, and past issues might be in bins or binders or available digitally. A librarian can help you find older issues—often going back many years!

Newspapers Most papers come out every day, so they have the most up-to-date coverage of what's happening now. Newspapers are also a great source for info that relates to the place they come from. Want to find out more about manatee migration, for example? Search a database for manatee stories from Florida newspapers.

Popular magazines These may cover a specific subject, such as food, cars, or pets. If you can find a magazine that matches your subject, use a database tool to search issues for the specific information you need.

Journals Find out what researchers and scholars have to say about your subject. These periodicals are usually for experts in a certain topic—such as doctors for a medical journal—so the writing may seem formal or technical. But journals can be a great source for data about a subject you're studying.

Online Info

The library can connect you to info that's often better than what you'll find by just searching the Internet.

Digital encyclopedias Many come from the same companies that make the big A-to-Z book encyclopedias in your classroom or school library. They have the same giant range of information—plus sounds, videos, and interactive features, too.

Subject databases From health info to consumer product reviews to family history facts and much, much more, the library can connect you to digital information you can't reach without the library's special access.

Online periodicals The library has digital tools for searching older issues of magazines and newspapers, so you can find info you need from periodicals that are no longer on the shelves. With your library card number, you may be able to use many of these sources right from your home computer. Check with your librarian to find out how.

ONLINE RESEARCH

Get the best results when you search the Internet.

The Internet is like the Wild West of information. It's a wide-open space, there aren't many rules, and anyone can put just about anything on it. This means you can't trust everything you find on the Internet to be true, correct, or up-to-date. So when you're researching your project, look for these clues to make sure a website is a solid source.

CREDENTIALS

Credentials are like qualifications. You want to use information from websites that are *qualified* to give it to you. Newspapers and magazines check their facts and can be held accountable for the information they provide. University research sites and government sites get checked, too. Look for the name of an author or publisher. Sites that don't come from a source you recognize or that don't list a qualified author or publisher may not have the most accurate information.

ADVERTISING

A site filled mostly with ads might be more concerned with selling you something than with providing accurate, current information.

GENERAL STORE

sources and links

Many of the best online sources let you know where they get *their* information. You might find a reference list of books, articles, and other sources somewhere on their site, or you might see links to other related websites. Check out the links. Are they current? Do they have credentials? These can be other good sources for your project.

presentation

Sometimes small signs can tell you a lot about a website's quality. Are there spelling and grammar errors or other kinds of obvious mistakes? Is the web page messy or too busy or hard to read? Is there a lot of flash? These are signs that a website has not been prepared by professionals with credentials or checked for standards of quality.

 ## TWO RULES FOR SAFE SEARCHING

1. Whether at home or school, never give out your name, address, phone number, or any other personal information online.

2. If a website or a person makes you uncomfortable, or if you feel something's not quite right, don't reply or comment, and do talk it over with your parents or an adult you trust. They can help steer you back to the information you need.

GET TO THE SOURCE

For the research projects below, decide whether information from each source is likely to be solid or shaky.

1. You're putting together a poster about zebras. You review . . .

an article from an online encyclopedia you access at your local library.

solid source   shaky source

a website called Kid-O-Pedia that seems to give some facts about zebras but also advertises zebra toys and doesn't list an author or publisher.

solid source   shaky source

a story on zebra habitats in a well-known wildlife magazine.

solid source   shaky source

2. You're working on a current events speech about a new law that Congress just passed. You consider information from . . .

a political opinion website where people post thoughts and complaints about Congress.

solid source   shaky source

a front-page article about the law from a national newspaper.

solid source   shaky source

a TV show that features celebrities arguing about politics.

solid source   shaky source

3. You're making a model of the Grand Canyon. You search for facts on . . .

the official government website of Grand Canyon National Park.

solid source   shaky source

your friend's aunt's social media post about her vacation there.

solid source   shaky source

the website of a university geography department whose scholars study the Grand Canyon.

solid source   shaky source

4. You're researching a service project for homeless cats. You click on . . .

the first website that pops up for "cats that need homes." (First on the list means most important, right?)

solid source   shaky source

the website of the Humane Society of the United States.

solid source   shaky source

a website called "#1 Kitten Lover" that has sooo many adorable pictures but looks like it was put together by a kid.

solid source   shaky source

answers

Did you choose the **blue** answers? Super! You know how to find reliable research material. Did you choose any **green?** It can be tricky to tell the difference between good sources and those that only *look* good, but with practice you'll be able to spot the ones you can rely on. First use your instincts and common sense. Then ask yourself these questions:

Is this a known source that is accountable for its information?

Is it an encyclopedia, established newspaper, government, or university? Is the publisher or author clearly identified? Does the information include its own sources with good credentials? Does the site *look* professional?

Is the information in this source fact or opinion?

You can use both! Just be sure you know the difference. A campaign advertisement for a political candidate will present different information (and may not be as factually reliable) as a newspaper article about him or her.

Is the information current?

Scientific information and news stories, in particular, should be as current as possible for the most up-to-date facts on changing subjects.

Take Note

Gather and organize the information from your sources—
and put the ideas in your own words.

Once you've found the books, websites, and other sources you need, take notes on the information you might use in your project.

NOTES...
Use a notebook, note cards, or a computer to take notes.

Jot down key facts and ideas—you don't need to write in complete sentences.

Use sticky notes to flag useful information in books—no writing or highlighting.

Print out online information, and highlight important ideas on the paper.

sources?
Check your assignment. Your teacher might want you to use different sources, such as one book and one website.

COPY SMART

Plagiarism is presenting the words or ideas of other people as your own. When writing a report or putting together a project, it's important to put ideas into your own words and to give credit when credit is due. These note-taking tips will help keep your projects plagiarism-free.

Keep track of what information comes from what source. As you're taking notes, write the title of each source above your notes about it. It's useful to make a note of the page numbers, too, so that you can find the information again. Also, your teacher may want you to provide page numbers.

Practice **paraphrasing.** Read your source material. Then set it aside while you make notes in your own words about the main ideas from the source.

When you copy information directly from a source into your research notes, put quotation marks around the information and write "QUOTE" next to it. When you use a direct quote in your project, put quotation marks around it and tell where it comes from.

from "Eiffel tower", Britannica School (online)
- designed by Gustave Eiffel
- built in 1889 for the Centennial Exposition, to mark 100 years since the French Revolution.
- 300 meters tall
- QUOTE: "Not until the Chrysler Building was completed in New York City in 1930 was there a taller structure in the world."

GIVING CREDIT

Whether you're writing a book report, building a model, or creating an experiment for the science fair, finish your project with a bibliography.

A **bibliography** is a list showing where you found the information you used. It's how you provide your own credentials. Check the assignment to see how your teacher wants you to list your sources. Teachers often give students a bibliography form to fill out, with examples for books, periodicals, and websites.

CREDIT TIPS

- For a report, your teacher will probably want you to include your bibliography as the final page. For a visual project, write or print your bibliography on a card and attach it to your poster or model.

- Your teacher or the assignment will tell you what order the references should be in. They may be listed by the kind of source—such as books, websites, and magazines—or they may be in alphabetical order.

- If you are creating your bibliography instead of filling out a form, begin the first line of each source at the left margin and then indent any extra lines—unless your teacher tells you to do it differently.

- Some of your sources may not have exactly the same information that your teacher asks for. Or maybe you can't tell what's what or how to find it. If you're not sure how to list a source, be sure to ask! Your teacher knows that it's not always easy, especially with online sources.

- Follow your teacher's directions for telling how certain kinds of sources are published. The details about book, newspaper, and website sources, for example, are all different.

- Remember photos! When you include a photo on a poster or in a report, add a small credit with the photographer's name directly below it.

Photo: E. M. Henke

Ms. Massey's Bibliography Sheet

Project Title:_____

Your Name:_____ Date: _____

Provide one source of each kind, and write the info as it's shown in the example.

BOOK

Author's last name, first name. Book Title. Where published: Publishing Company,
   Copyright year. (Page numbers you read)

Richards, Mary. A Smart Girl's Guide to Everything. Midtown, WI: Live and Learn, 2014.
   (Pages 5-12, 37-62)

WEBPAGE OR WEBSITE

"Title of Page or Site." URL. (Date you found it)

"Life in the Desert." www.lifeontheblueplanet.org/desert-animals. (March 14, 2017)

ONLINE DATABASE OR ENCYCLOPEDIA

"Article or Page Title." Database Title. Date published. (Date you found it)

"The Eiffel Tower." Universe Encyclopedia Online. 2004. (March 5, 2017)

PRINT ENCYCLOPEDIA

"Article Title." Encyclopedia Title, volume, page numbers. Date published.

"Architecture." Earth Book, volume A, pages 194-195. 2014.

MAGAZINE OR NEWSPAPER ARTICLE

"Article Title." Magazine or Newspaper Title, page numbers. Date published.

"City to Build a New School." The Highland Post, pages 3-4. April 17, 2016.

PERSONAL INTERVIEW

Last name of person interviewed, first name. Personal interview. Date of interview.

Bickner, Marcia. Personal interview. December 10, 2016.

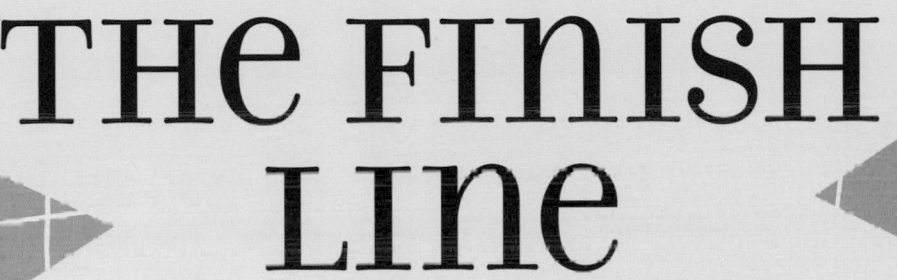

THE FINISH LINE

Polish your project, work with a team, and solve project problems.

CHECK IT OUT

Before the due date, give your project a final review with the help of these handy checklists.

CHECKLIST

The Basics

* Did I meet all the requirements of my assignment?
* Did I format my project the way my teacher wanted?
* Did I include a title, my name, and the date?

Information

* Is the main idea of my project clear?
* Is my information accurate?
* Did I include my sources or bibliography?

Presentation

* Is my project neat and easy to read?
* Is my project sturdy enough to be moved and displayed, if needed?
* Did I check grammar, spelling, capitalization, and punctuation?
* Am I prepared for my speech? Did I practice?

Team UP

Make the most of project partners! Answer these questions to find out where you fit on a school project team.

1. The classroom job you'd likely choose is . . .

a. class secretary: You'd take notes at class meetings and keep a calendar of important due dates.

b. line leader: You're ready to take charge and make sure your class gets around school without wasting time.

c. pencil patrol: You're happy to check each day to make sure the class has a steady supply of sharpened pencils.

2. When your family cooks a special meal together, you like to . . .

a. chop the veggies and stir.

b. make the grocery list and figure out how all the dishes can get done at the same time.

c. choose the recipes!

3. You and your pals are planning a surprise party for a friend. You'd add to the celebration by . . .

a. helping with food and decorations.

b. planning the guest list and mailing invitations.

c. choosing the party theme and assigning your friends to make food and plan games.

4. You love soccer. Your teammates know they can count on you to . . .

a. motivate and inspire the team.

b. give your best effort at every practice and game.

c. keep an up-to-date team schedule and work with parents to organize carpools for practices.

5. In the school yearbook, your classmates vote you . . .

a. most organized.

b. most reliable.

c. best leader.

GO TEAM ★

answers

Did you select **pink** answers most? You might make a great coach for your project group. You're a natural leader, and you know how to listen to everyone's ideas, inspire them, and guide your group along the path to success.

Did you pick several **purples?** You're a true team player. You don't see some project jobs as being more important than others— you see work that needs to get done, and you pitch in wherever you can. You're a real asset to any school project group.

Did you go for **greens** the most? You may be a great administrator. Every project group needs someone to keep track of schedules and details. You'll make sure your group gets everything done on time and in top shape.

Why do teachers assign group projects? Because working in a group helps you learn to get along with different types of people. It helps you listen to others and build on their ideas. The teamwork know-how you get from group projects today will come in handy your whole life through!

partner problems

What can you do when one of your project partners won't go along with the group?

Bossy pants

You make the poster. Give it to me tomorrow. Make it look great!

You go to the library and find 10 books.

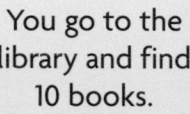

I'm writing the report. You do the research, but I'll put it together.

Try saying . . .

I'm glad you're so excited to get started! Hey, I have an idea. Before we decide who's doing what, why don't we each say what job we're most interested in and what we'd feel best doing?

Free agent

Here's my George Washington costume! Don't you love my wig?

But Grace, you were supposed to make a map of the 13 colonies!

Try saying . . .

Wow, that's so creative! When do you think you'll have the colonies map ready? We're hoping to pull everything together by tomorrow.

Later Gator

Do you have your photos for the collage?

I'll get them. The project's not due till tomorrow, you know!

Try saying . . .

We were hoping to put the finishing touches on the collage tonight. Could you bring the photos over after school? I can't wait to see what you picked!

HOW TO BE AN A+ PROJECT PARTNER

Listening

Make sure all group members get the chance to share their ideas and opinions. When others are talking, pay attention to what they have to say. If you're waiting for your turn to talk and thinking of what you want to say, you might miss something good.

Compromise

When you're working in a group, make decisions that are best for the group instead of any individual members—whether it's your BFF, a squeaky wheel, or even you.

Honoring strengths

Give the drawing project to the girl who loves art. Ask the winner of the spelling bee to proofread your poster. When each person does a job she's confident she can do well, your project will shine its brightest.

Commitment

Make a vow to stick to deadlines, show up for group meetings, and do anything else you're signed up to do. You are all counting on one another to get the job done. Shake on it!

LAST-MINUTE MELTDOWN?

Your project is due tomorrow . . .

How would you handle this tricky situation? Follow the flowchart to find out.

START

It's 4 p.m. the day before your project is due. You're not finished—not even close—and you've got soccer practice at 4:30. What should you do? You decide to . . .

pass on practice and take a good look at what you have done so far—and what you still need to do.

skip practice—just for today—and fly through the work you have left.

REPORT

You've looked through your work. Your report is half written. You decide to put your efforts toward . . .

You've put together a poster. It's not pretty, but it will have to do. Next, for your report you . . .

go to practice. You've got a big game Saturday, and you can stay up late to finish the project.

After practice, you finally settle down to work. You begin by . . .

reading through the half-written report—then crumpling it up! It's awful! You've got to start over.

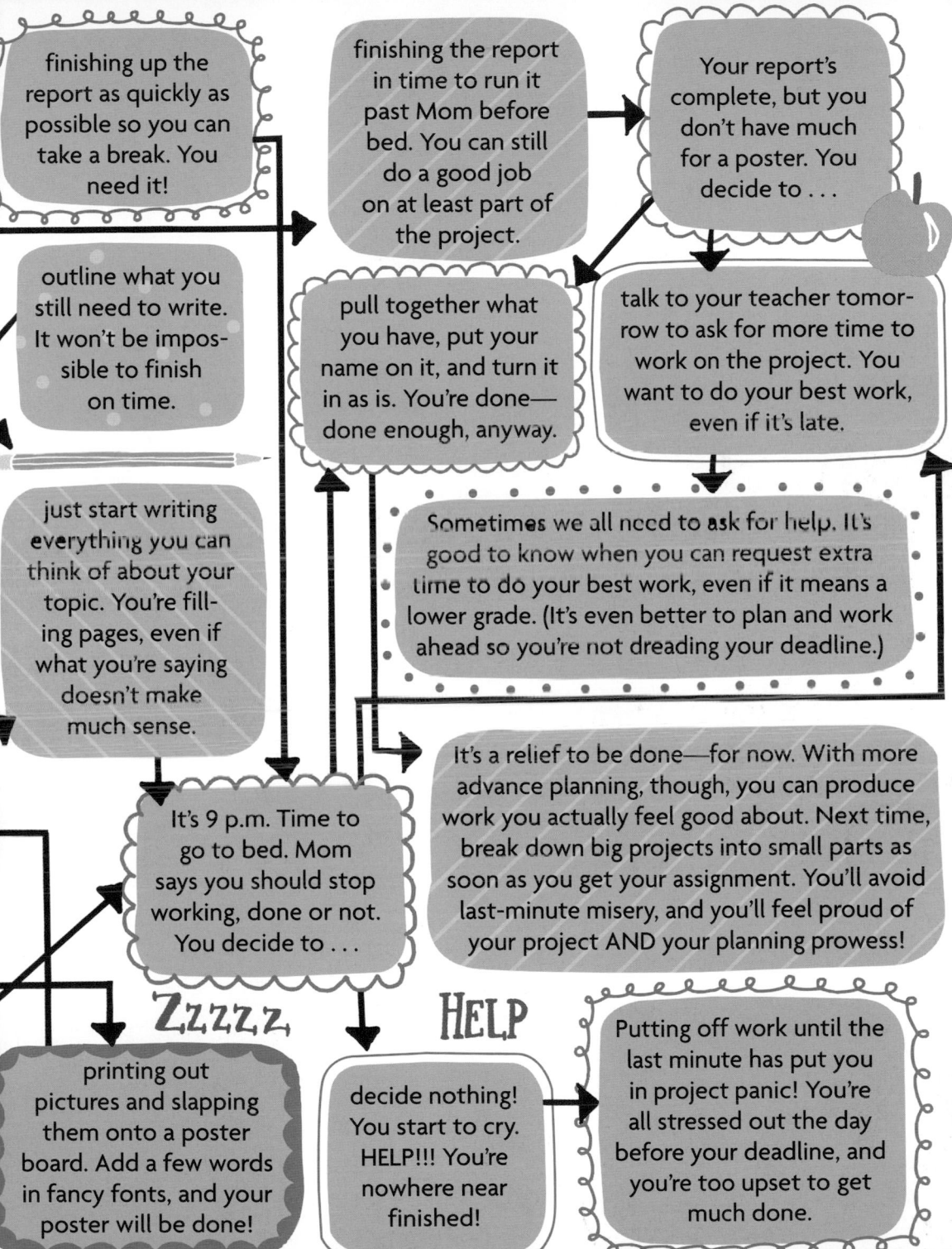

κeep calm and carry on

Did the flowchart stress you out?

The stress from reading it is probably nothing compared to the real-life pressure girls put on themselves when they put off a project! If you find yourself facing a last-minute meltdown, here are a few ways you can help yourself manage.

Take a deep breath. Try to stay calm to make good use of the time you do have.

Make a list. Write down what you've done. Write what you still need to do.

Scale down your project. Build a model that's 12 inches tall, not four feet.

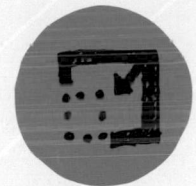

Just keep working! Don't be distracted by friends, family, TV, or your phone.

Go to bed if it's late. You can't do your best when you're exhausted. Check your progress and make a plan in the morning.

Talk to your teacher. Be honest about what you still need to do. Ask for partial credit, more time to complete your work—or both.

HELPING HANDS— OR NOT?

It's tempting to get help from your parents, especially when the project is big or you're falling behind.

Your parents want you to do your best. And many kinds of help make your project more fun or help you learn. But help can go too far. Where is the line between parents helping and parents hijacking your homework?

1. You're creating a crossword puzzle with the names of world explorers for history class. You decide to . . .

   a. let your mom try the puzzle to check if it's correct.

   b. let your mom come up with the clues. You listed the explorers' names and fit them together in the puzzle. That was the hard part!

2. You're supposed to dress up like a character from your favorite book. You choose *Charlotte's Web*—and you'll dress like Wilbur. When you tell your dad about the project, he wants to help. He loves that book! You let him . . .

   a. sew a complete pig outfit. He's a whiz with the sewing machine, and he always makes the best Halloween costumes.

   b. help you dye an old pillowcase pink and cut holes for your head and arms. You've got a pink turtleneck to wear underneath, and you can make a cute pig nose and ears from pink paper.

3. You're building a model of a settler's cabin. Your mom sits down to chat as you work, but pretty soon she's changing your design, saying your building could be stronger. You say . . .

   a. "Thanks, Mom! I know you're an engineer, but I really should build this on my own."

   b. "Thanks, Mom! I know you're an engineer. You can probably build this in a flash."

4. For the science fair, you're testing which design of paper airplane flies the farthest. Your dad's a master at making them. You ask for a bit of help, and then you let him . . .

   a. teach you to fold a few cool designs.

   b. choose which designs to make and fold all the planes for you.

5. You're making a poster featuring your favorite athlete, Serena Williams. You ask your mom to take a look. She says you need to work on the lettering you're using for the title and labels. Pretty soon your mom is . . .

   a. writing all your headings in cool letters made of tennis racket shapes. She's a fantastic artist!

   b. helping you choose a clear font so you can print out all the headings for your poster, cut them out, and paste them on.

answers

Did you choose any **gold?** Watch out! Don't expect or allow your parents to take over your work when you ask for a hand on a project. Sure, your architect mom can build a better model skyscraper than you can, and your writer dad can pen a perfect book report. But if your parents do your work, you're not really learning. Plus, teachers know when students' work is not their own. And you'll know, too. So be clear with yourself and your parents that you really appreciate their help, but you need to do the project. They'll be proud you did—and so will you.

A WINNING LINE-UP

The right kind of help can make your project even stronger. Here's how to ask for it.

getting organized

Ask your teacher, "I have lots of ideas and I've started my research, but I'm not sure what to focus on. Could you please help me organize my ideas and choose the best direction?"

editing and proofreading

Ask a parent: "My project is finished! I've looked it over carefully, but do you have time to take a look before I print it out?"

finding information

Ask a librarian, "I'm looking for information about the Eiffel Tower. I need to write a report and build a model. Could you please help me find the best sources?"

collecting supplies

Ask a parent, "Could you please drive me to the store? I need paint and poster board for my map project."

Don't wait too long before you ask for help. Give yourself—and the people whose help you need—plenty of time. They'll be especially happy to do it if you remember to say . . .

THANK YOU!

Congratulations

You're officially a Project Pro!

You're ready to face any
school project assignment!

You'll always . . .

- ♥ read the directions
- ♥ make a plan
- ♥ get organized
- ♥ research right
- ♥ be creative

and

- ♥ be project PROUD!

Do you have a project tip or triumph to share?

Write to us!
School RULES! Projects Editor
American Girl
8400 Fairway Place
Middleton, WI 53562

Here are some other American Girl® books you might like.

Each sold separately. Find more books online at americangirl.com.

Parents, request a FREE catalogue at **americangirl.com/catalogue.**
Sign up at **americangirl.com/email** to receive the latest news and exclusive offers.

Discover online games, quizzes, activities,
and more at **americangirl.com/play**